THE
NATURAL WAY
TO MUSIC

Best wishes Tom —
Bill Keith

The Natural Way To Music

Jim D'Ville & Bill Keith

Natural Way Music
P.O. Box 203 Yachats, Oregon   97498
Printed in the United States of America

ISBN# 1-888934-05-0
Library of Congress Control Number: 2003106668
First Printing August 2001
Second Printing June 2003
Third Printing April 2004

Cover Design by Linda Grist D'Ville

Dedicated to my sister,
Ramona Kay Turbeville,
who bequeathed the love
of music to me.

Special thanks to:
Bill Keith, Susie Davis,
Richard Greene, Jess Smith,
Linda Grist D'Ville and all
the musicians, students and
friends who have helped
along the way.

Jim D'Ville

My heartfelt thanks:
To my parents for encouraging
my interest in music; to Pete
Seeger, Don Stover, Don Reno,
Earl Scruggs, Tony Trischka,
Béla Fleck and the many other
banjo players who have inspired
me over the years; to Jim D'Ville
and Linda Grist D'Ville for their
invaluable help in the preparation
of this book.

Bill Keith

Visit our website: www.naturalwaymusic.com

Contents

Introduction
Your Musical Instrument   i
The Journey   ii
Learning to Listen   iii

Part One   1
The Major Scale   3
Intervals   8
Chords   12
The Tones, Then The Tunes   16

Part Two   17
Circle of Fifths   19
The Modes   24
The Tri-Tone   30
Pentatonic Scale   32
Chord Progressions   34
Minor Scales   36
Summary   39

Part Three-Appendix   40
Popular Scale Patterns   41
Index of Major Scales   42
Scales & Arpeggios   44
Solfege Songs   45
Holiday Tunes   48
A Note on Notation   53
Glossary   54
Suggested Reading   55

All sidebar quotes by Bill Keith

Your Musical Instrument

The first musical instrument is the voice, and it usually comes as standard equipment with the human body. We use it to speak, make all kinds of interesting sounds, and to sing. It is our built-in musical instrument and we can use it to tune-in to the notes created by other instruments.

If you don't yet have an instrument other than your voice, here are some suggestions. An inexpensive electronic keyboard is a great instrument to hear the tones and visually see the notes (keys) you'll be learning laid out in a linear fashion.

An easy stringed instrument to get started on is the ukulele. The ukulele is great for getting your knowledge of chord progressions going and playing songs right away. Simple flutes like the Irish tin whistle are another inexpensive way to get started hearing musical tones.

If you're just starting out, don't make a major financial commitment by purchasing an expensive instrument right away. Start simple, and as your musical knowledge grows you will find the perfect instrument to express your musical creativity.

The Journey

Have you ever heard the wind whistling through the trees? Can you whistle or hum? There is no special talent required to hearing sounds, or producing them yourself. We all possess these innate musical talents that we use everyday. Whether we realize it or not, we are all musicians.

We can build upon this innate ability by learning the twelve tones of the musical alphabet, and the musical grammar of their usage. No one ever learned to read and write without first learning the alphabet. Becoming familiar with the language of music also affords you the ability to communicate with other musicians which is invaluable when playing with others. And while many people spend years in school studying music theory, the overly academic nature of the approach leaves many people scratching their heads. Luckily, you've found the short course!

Begin your journey on *The Natural Way To Music* with no expectations. They are not needed. No musician ever knows where the music will lead.

"We all learned how to talk and carry on a conversation before we learned to read and write. Musically, not everyone wants to take that leap to learn the musical grammar."

Learning to Listen

Just as an artist learns to see in a very detailed way, a musician learns to hear tones in a very specific way. The artist trains the eyes, the musician trains the ears.

People who say they can't draw no doubt haven't spent the time learning to see and then transferring the images to paper or canvas. Studying music relies on a similar principle; learning to hear and identify specific musical sounds and transferring them to a musical instrument.

An artist studies perspective, line, form, and light and shadow to acquire the skills needed to accurately create two-dimensional images. A musician studies tonal relationships and rhythm to expand their palette of available musical elements needed to create songs.

Once you begin to program these tonal relationships into your mind, ears, and fingers the magic comes into play. You'll realize you are already familiar with a lot of the information presented in this book because you've heard these patterns, structure and form in the music you've been listening to your entire life. These are the musical elements that make up your favorites songs!

Take your time with this material, and with patient practice the wonderful mysteries of becoming a musician will be revealed.

"When we wake up each morning none of us has a script of exactly what we're going to say that day. We make it up as we go along. Music can be like that too. Get a good handle on the musical vocabulary and you can make the music up as you go along. That's called improvising."

1 Part One

If this were a book about learning how to run a 26-mile marathon race the first exercise would not be to go out and run 26 miles. It might simply be to take a brisk walk around the block. Large goals are achieved through small steps.

The **Major Scale** is composed of small musical steps. As you begin using this book, remember that each step in the musical staircase is important. Don't skip over steps thinking you will reach the top of the staircase quicker.

In Part One you'll not only be learning basic music principles, you will also be developing your "ear-hand" coordination. That's why playing and listening to the exercises and examples is so important.

As you become familiar with the sounds of the notes found in the Major Scale you'll begin to recognize the two-note tonal relationships discussed in the **Intervals** chapter.

Singing the solfege syllables as you practice is also an essential element to strengthening ear-hand coordination and internalizing musical intervals.

"Learning all depends on your attitude. You'll see someone else playing something on an instrument which seems difficult and you may say, 'Boy, that looks hard, I'll never be able to do that.' Don't predict your own future that way. I'd rather you say to yourself, 'Hey, if they can do it, so can I. I'll just take my time and I'll get there too.'"

Continuing up the staircase of musical knowledge you'll come to the chapter on **Chords**, which begins with three-note tonal relationships.

Each step in your trip up the musical staircase builds on the previous one which is why it is important to fully understand the step you are on before moving on to the next one.

The greatest benefit to learning general music principles in the manner presented here is you'll be absorbing the musical fundamentals and patterns used to create all western music, including country and western! This is what makes the ascent up the musical staircase so exciting. You are learning to play whatever your ears want to hear.

By taking this step in your musical journey you have embarked on a noble endeavor, the direction of which may change at any time, whose outcome is unknown and can not be predicted. How exciting!

Getting Started
Watch the movie *The Sound of Music* and sing along with Julie Andrews as she teaches the Von Trapp children how to sing using the solfege syllables.

The Major Scale

There's only one!

The best thing about the Major Scale is that you already know the sound of it! That's what makes humming along with a song you may never have heard before so easy.

In the movie *The Sound of Music*, Julie Andrews sings the notes of the Major Scale in the song *Do, Re, Mi (Doe a Deer)*. Well, what she is actually doing is singing a song based on what are known as solfege (sohl-FEZH) syllables, or single syllable names associated with each note of the Major Scale. Why do people sing the notes using the solfege syllables? To associate a vocal sound for each step of the scale, thus providing a reference in distinguishing how far apart the tones are from each other in the scale.

There is only one Major Scale pattern for all twelve keys. Let's consider that Major Scale pattern as the first song in our repertoire. The millions of other songs are simply melodies with the solfege sounds mixed up.

The notes of the Major Scale can be considered musical neighbors that share basic tonal relationships. So, let's meet the neighbors!

"We have to learn where songs live - - the Major Scale is the place to start."

"These are the notes we have heard since we were born. Musically, we already know these notes, which puts a lot of the work behind us."

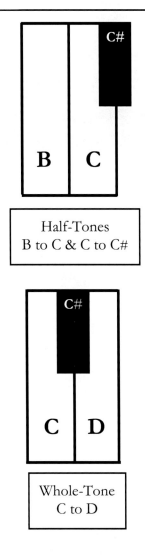

Half-Tones
B to C & C to C#

Whole-Tone
C to D

The Major Scale is composed of musical building blocks that come in two sizes, the *Half-Tone* and the *Whole-Tone* (also called *Half-steps* and *Whole-steps*).

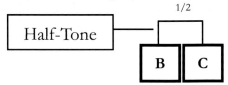

Two *Half-Tones* create one *Whole-Tone*.

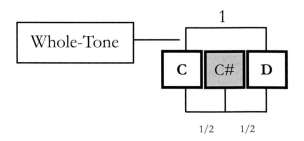

This combination of whole-tones and half-tones combine to create the Major Scale pattern. In the key of C, the pattern lays out naturally on the white keys of a piano keyboard starting on the note C. Adjacent keys on the keyboard, including both black and white, are one half-step apart.

C Major Scale Pattern

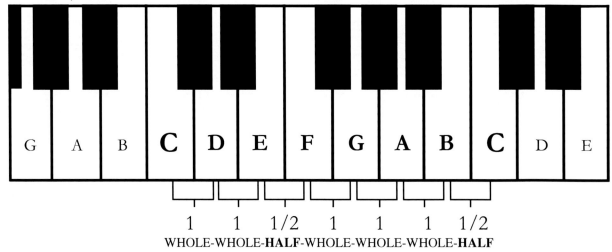

Start on C and count up the Major Scale using the **1 - 1 - 1/2 - 1 - 1 - 1 - 1/2** pattern. You'll notice the first seven letters of the alphabet (**A - B - C - D - E - F - G**) are used to name the musical notes.

Major Scale
Pattern

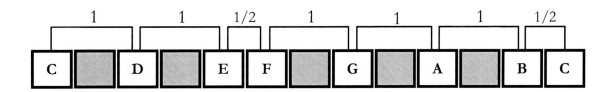

Just as the notes on the piano keyboard are one half-step apart, successive frets on a fretted instrument are one half-step apart. As you can see on the fingerboard diagram below, moving two frets will change the pitch by one whole step.

Major Scale Pattern – Stringed Instrument Fingerboard

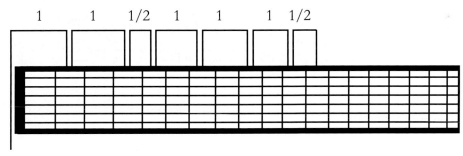

Open String

This is a good time to experiment with finding the Major Scale pattern on your instrument. If you have a stringed instrument, first play the pattern on one string (open, 2nd fret, 4th fret, 5th fret, etc.). Then play the scale using more than one string.

"It's always best to get acquainted with musical ideas first by their sound."

Ear Training
Practice listening to the whole-step/half-step intervals with your eyes closed. The eyes are always competing with the ears.

There are no black keys between B and C, and E and F on a piano keyboard which means these notes are one half-step apart. Play the white keys of a piano from left to right starting on C and you've played a C Major Scale.

If you sing the solfege syllables (Do-Re-Mi-Fa-Sol-La-Ti-Do) as you play each note you'll reap added benefits. Look what it did for Julie Andrews.

C Major Scale

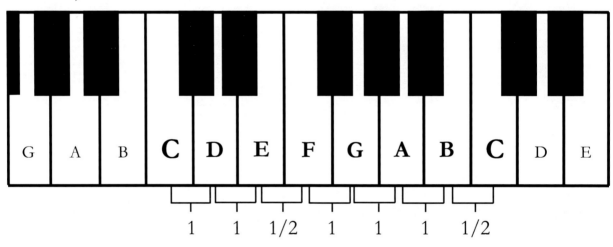

1	1	1/2	1	1	1	1/2

"The seven notes of the Major Scale are like the seven days of the week. If 'Do' is Sunday, it will repeat the following Sunday one octave higher."

Also try playing the notes of a C Major Scale randomly and listen to the tones produced. Feel free to experiment with how the tones sound played in a different order.

The Major Scale is a portable pattern we can take with us to play in other keys. Since the key of C Major is the only key played just on the white keys, we'll need to use the black keys, the sharps and flats, to play in other musical keys.

The piano keyboard is a great place to learn about the black keys, and how this whole business of sharps (#) and flats (♭) works.

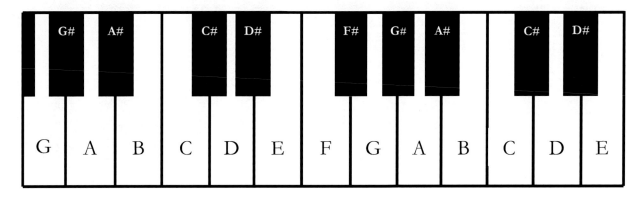

Start on the first G note on the keyboard above and count up using the Major Scale pattern. You'll see the first half-step falls correctly between B and C. But, to complete the pattern so the second half-step falls in the correct position, one black key is needed, F# (F sharp). The key of G Major has one sharp, F#.

To play in the key of D you'll need two sharps to complete the pattern, F# and C#.And, for the key of A, three sharps are needed, F#, C#, and G#. **Now, try finding the pattern to other keys on the diagram above, or, better yet, on your instrument.**

Finding the Major Scale in any key is easy. Choose a note to start on, apply the Major Scale whole-step/half-step pattern, sing the Do-Re-Mi…, and let your ears confirm that the notes fit the pattern.

Ear Training
Play a Major Scale pattern on your instrument. Then, play the Major Scale pattern in a different key. Just start on a new note.

"This (solfege) is useful to me when I'm listening to something and I don't know what key it's in. I find the 'Do' in it, or the harmonic center, and then use the syllables since I know they will work the same in all keys."

Intervals
The Spaces Between The Notes

"Major and minor are just other words for big and little, like the Major League and the Minor League."

Playing Major Scale intervals is like hopping up and down a musical staircase. An interval is the distance between two tones, or steps, in the scale (Do-Re, Do-Mi, Do-Fa, etc.). **Play each Major Scale interval on your instrument.** Hum each two-note set, or sing the notes using the solfege syllables (see exercise on opposite page). These are the building blocks of melody. Get to know their sounds.

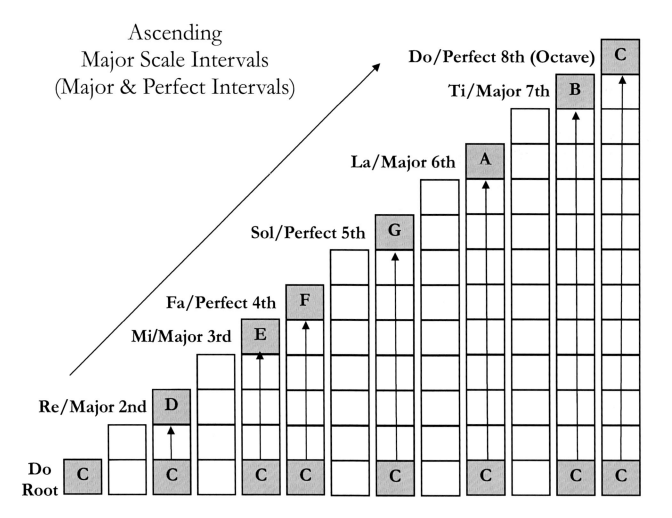

Ascending Major Scale Intervals (Major & Perfect Intervals)

There are three basic types of intervals, Major, minor, and Perfect. Each has a different sound quality. Major intervals sound relaxed and even, while minor intervals sound a bit uneasy. Perfect intervals, which are the easiest for our ears to recognize, have a strong and stable sound.

The intervals of the Perfect 4th and Perfect 5th share a special relationship to Do (the tonic note of the scale). In C Major, the Perfect 4th is C to F, and the Perfect 5th is C to G. Each note in these intervals can be found the others' scale. For example, F is in

C D E **F** **G** A B		
F G A Bb **C** D E **G** A B **C** D E F#		

the C Major Scale, and C is in the F Major Scale. G is in the C Major Scale, and C is in the G Major Scale. None of the other notes in the C Major Scale share this perfect relationship. Try it with another note from the C Major Scale. D is in the C Major Scale, however, C is not in the D Major Scale, C# is.

Allow your ears to absorb the sound of these musical relationships. You'll find your ears know these sounds and the intervals between them better than you may think. By playing, singing, and listening to these intervals you are linking your fingers to your ears. Your brain is simply acting as a processing unit. It's like learning to whistle a tune with your fingers.

1-8	Do	Do
1-7	Do	Ti
1-6	Do	La
1-5	Do	Sol
1-4	Do	Fa
1-3	Do	Mi
1-2	Do	Re

Ear Training
Play and sing the intervals above. Start with Do-Re at the bottom, and ascend the scale. Once you reach Do-Do, descend the scale, Do-Ti, Do-La, etc. Next, try mixing them up, Fa-Ti, Sol-La, etc.

Intervals	# 1/2 Steps
Perfect 8th	12
Major 7th	11
Major 6th	9
Perfect 5th	7
Perfect 4th	5
Major 3nd	4
Major 2nd	2

Chromatic Scale

Chromatic Scale
Pattern

When you play all twelve half-steps consecutively it's called a *Chromatic Scale.* **Play the notes of the C Chromatic scale on your instrument.**

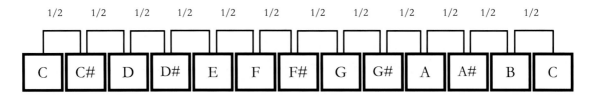

1/2	1/2	1/2	1/2	1/2	1/2	1/2	1/2	1/2	1/2	1/2	1/2

C | C# | D | D# | E | F | F# | G | G# | A | A# | B | C

Solfege Songs

Teasing In Solfege
As a child, you may have heard the expression, "Nah-nah, nah-nah, nah, nah." In solfege that popular taunt translates to "Sol-Sol, Mi-La, Sol, Mi." Try it on the neighborhood children!

Playing different intervals may prompt familiar melodies to come to mind. Here's where the fun comes in. You are discovering where songs live. Get to know the intervals. Make them your friends and every time they come around in a tune you'll recognize them. Try singing the melodies below and finding the sounds on your instrument. Sing the **bold** face notes one octave lower.

London Bridge
Sol La-Sol Fa Mi Fa Sol,
Re Mi Fa, Mi Fa Sol...

Old MacDonald
Do Do Do **Sol La La Sol**,
Mi Mi Re Re Do.

There are more solfege song examples in the Appendix.

Yankee Doodle
Do Do Re Mi Do Mi Re **Sol**
Do Do Re Mi Do, **Ti**...

Intervals In The Chromatic Scale

Descending Solfege (phonetically spelled)		
8/Perfect 8th	DOE	DOE
7/Major 7th	TEE	TEE
#6-b7 minor 7th	LEE	TAY
6/Major 6th	LAH	LAH
#5-b6 minor 6th	SEE	LAY
5/Perfect 5th	SOL	SOL
*#4-b5 Aug.4-Dim.5	FEE	SAY
4/Perfect 4th	FAH	FAH
3/Major 3rd	MEE	MEE
#2-b3 minor 3rd	REE	MAY
2/Major 2nd	RAY	RAY
#1-b2 minor 2nd	DEE	RAH
1/Root	DOE	DOE

Scale Degree Interval Names

Ascending Solfege (phonetically spelled)

Ear Training

Play and sing the notes of the *Chromatic Scale* ascending and descending using the solfege syllables. These are all the notes we have. Get to know them!

"The intervals I first learned to recognize were octaves, fifths, and fourths. Later, I could recognize more; major thirds, minor thirds. As I got more familiar with it I could say, yeah, that's a major chord, that's a minor, or, I'm not sure what that chord is, it's something else, so I'd go back for more information."

*Augmented 4th/Diminished 5th (Augmented means raise a note one half-step, diminished means lower a note one half-step).

Chords

The Stacking of Intervals

Ascend the scale in rhythm by accenting the notes on the downbeat or foot-tap. When you count "One and Two and Three and Four," the numbers fall on the foot-tap and the *Ands* are counted as the foot rises.

What do firewood and intervals have in common? Firewood is stacked in cords and *Chords* are stacked intervals. A chord is a group of notes played simultaneously. In songs, chords harmonize with, or compliment the melody notes.

Major chords are built by playing the 1st, 3rd & 5th notes of a Major Scale together. Ascend the scale in rhythm and the 1st, 3rd & 5th notes of the Major Scale are projected on the downbeat (foot-tap).

C Major Chord:

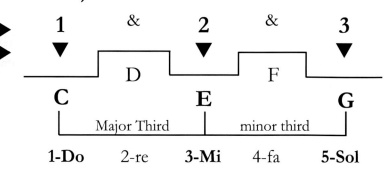

Anatomy Tip
Think of the five fingers on your right hand as the first five notes of a Major Scale. The thumb, middle, and little fingers are the 1, 3, & 5 notes of a Major Chord. Try it on a piano in the key of C.

G Major Chord:

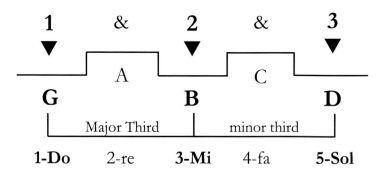

Two intervals stack up to form a Major chord. From the 1st to the 3rd note of a Major Scale is four half-steps, a Major Third. From the 3rd to the 5th is three half-steps, a minor third. When you play a Major chord the sound of the Major Third is projected (our ears want to hear the low, or, bottom interval of the stack). Flatting (lowering) the third note one half-step inverts the two intervals, projecting the minor third sound. **Play a Major chord on your instrument and then a minor chord. Hear the difference?**

C minor Chord:

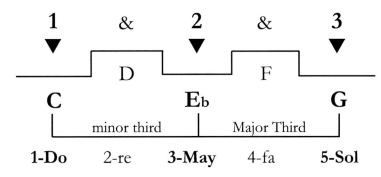

G minor Chord:

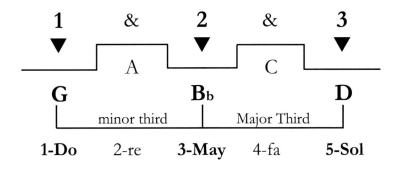

Listening to Major and minor chords trains your ears to hear Major and minor 3rd intervals.

Rhythm Helper
Rhythm; the tapping of a foot, the beat of a drum, or the click of a metronome, all help us keep time. Use your innate sense of rhythm (or a metronome) to play all the exercises and examples in even time. As Mr. Welk used to say, "An' a one, an' a two…"

"I thought things were hard when I started learning formulas and counting half-steps to find chords. But, when you start in the scale and go up in rhythm, the notes on the beat form the chord and it drops right out."

Diatonic Chords

Ear Training
Ascend the C Diatonic Chords in order. Listen to the relationship of each chord to the next and discover how *Lean On Me* was written!

Rudolph, The Diatonic Reindeer
Descend the Diatonic Chords from the octave on your instrument and find the names of Santa's reindeer!

The Major Scale is also known as the *Diatonic Scale.* The two identical four-note patterns of the Major Scale (Do-Re-Mi-Fa & Sol-La-Ti-Do) are called *Tetrachords,* each with its own tonic (also called root note). A Diatonic Scale can be thought of as a scale with two tonics; Do being the first tonic and Sol the second.

We can find a chord for every note in the Diatonic Scale. Start on C and play the first five notes in rhythm. The notes projected on the downbeat will be the 1-3-5 (Do-Mi-Sol) of the C Major chord (C-E-G). Now, start on D. You'll hear the notes D-F-A projected on the downbeat which produces a D minor chord (the 1-b3-5 notes of a D Major Scale).

Notice how the half-steps between B and C, and E and F shift toward the root in each ascending scale thus creating the new chords.

Diatonic Chords
Key of C Major

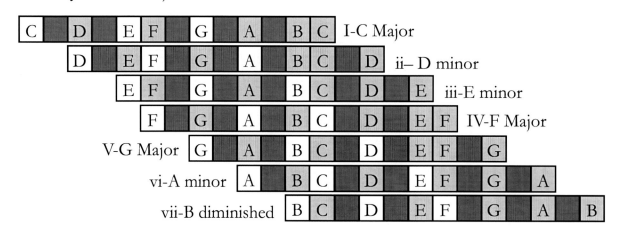

The chords that occur in the scales built on the 1st, 4th and 5th scale degrees are Major chords. That's why songs that use two or three Major chords utilize chord progressions with the I, IV, & V chords.

Similarly, songs with minor chords often use the ii, iii & vi chords. That's because those are the chords that naturally drop out of the scale on the downbeat when the scale is ascended in rhythm.

The resulting chord built from the 7th scale degree is a half-diminished chord (1-♭3-♭5-♭7).

Four-Note 7th Chords

You can build four-note chords by ascending the scale to the 7th note, which also falls on the downbeat. For example, starting on C, the 1st, 3rd, 5th, & 7th notes form a C Major Seventh Chord.

*A fully Diminished B Chord contains the chord tones B-D-F-A♭ (1-♭3-♭5-♭♭7).

Diatonic Chords In Any Key
Every note in every Major Scale has a chord associated with it. Just follow the downbeat!

"All the chords in this family, be they Major, minor, diminished, or 7ths, are all formed using the notes of the parent Major Scale."

What Chord Do I Play Here?
Let the melody guide you!

Diatonic
7th Chords
Key of C Major

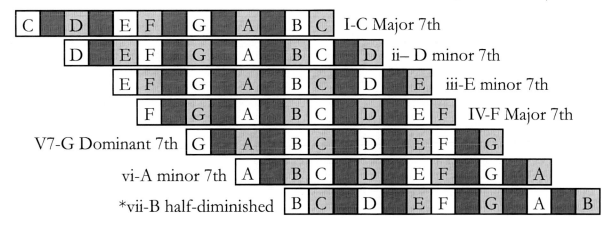

"Learn one procedure instead of memorizing a thousand results."

Ear Training
Play any note on your instrument. Hum along with the note. Remember what that note sounds like. Hum the note from memory. Now, play the note on your instrument to re-enforce the sound. Hum along with the note again. Say its name. Make this routine a part of your practice and soon you'll be able to recognize each of the twelve tones just as you recognize the sound of a familiar voice.

The Tones, Then The Tunes

As you practice, let each scale, interval and chord tone drift easily into your ears and lodge in your mind. The closer you listen, the more you'll begin to hear. As you become more familiar with the tones, their relationships with one another will become more apparent. Soon you'll find the tones are beginning to lead you around by the ears.

The first thing most everyone wants to do when they decide to take up a musical instrument is play songs, up to speed, today! They want to put the songs before the tones. The tones, or notes, are what songs are composed of, so a patient study of their sound and musical relationships gives us a logical place to begin the study of music.

Part Two of *The Natural Way To Music* will provide you with many insights as to how this family of tones called the Major Scale operates. Their relationships, patterns, and inner workings will reveal a logical understanding why music does what it does.

2 Part Two

Once you have a working knowledge of the basic functions of the Major Scale, its Intervals and the building of Chords, you are ready to move on to this section of the book. As you've already learned, there is only one Major Scale pattern, however, there are many keys, or pitches, and other scales in which you may play.

Using the **Circle of Fifths,** you'll discover that when you learn something about one key, the same knowledge will apply to all eleven other keys! You'll also find many useful shortcuts which will make it easier to play in all keys.

The chapter on **The Modes** reveals how easy it is to play in unique sounding keys using the Major Scale notes you already know.

In the **Tri-Tone** chapter you'll learn about the all-important musical elements known as tension and resolution, which motivates chords to resolve back to the root chord.

The five-note **Pentatonic Scale** is really just the Major Scale with the tension and resolution factor removed. It is one of the most widely utilized scales in the world. It's found in old-time, Asian, blues, and liturgical music, and many popular Christmas songs.

"There's more than one right way to play something. We want to get to the point where we improvise, where we make things up. We have to learn about where songs live, and that's the key that they're in and the things that happen in that key."

The chapter on **Chord Progressions** reveals how songs naturally progress from one chord to another and their motivation for doing so.

And finally, the **Minor Scales** chapter demonstrates the relationships that exist between the Natural, Harmonic and Melodic Minor Scales.

As you begin this section of the book remember to pace yourself, moving on to the next step only after you have a firm understanding of the step you are on. **Always experiment on your instrument with the information presented.** Do the exercises in the book, and make up your own exercises. Learn to practice effectively by setting small, accomplishable goals.

You may come across something in Part Two that will require a pencil and a piece of paper to figure out. We all learn in different ways. Find the way that is right for you, and don't be afraid to mark up this book with a pencil. That's what it's for!

Circle Of Fifths

The Musical Universe

The Circle of Fifths is like a clock with the letters of the musical alphabet evenly spaced around it.

Circle of 4ths?
If you go counter-clockwise on the Circle of 5ths, it becomes a Circle of 4ths (C up to F, F up to Bb, etc.).

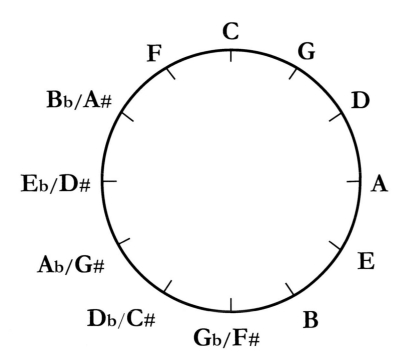

Reading the Circle of Fifths is like telling time. The numbers on a clock are spaced five minutes apart and the letters on the Circle of Fifths are spaced a *Fifth Interval* apart. Start on the C note and move clockwise to the next letter, G, and you have moved up a Fifth (do-sol). D is a Fifth up from G, A is a Fifth up from D and so on. The pattern continues all the way around the circle back to C. **Start on C, and play each note of the Circle of Fifths going around the circle clockwise.**

"This is the musical universe. These are all the notes we have, so every chord, every melody, everything musical has got to be here one place or another. It's how you look at it."

Masking off the notes which have sharps and flats (the black piano keys) leaves the white notes showing which make up the C Major Scale.

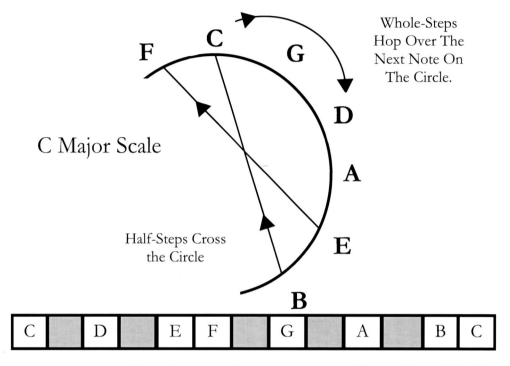

C Major Scale

C		D		E	F		G		A		B	C

Starting at the root note C at 12 o'clock, count up the scale. You'll notice the whole steps hop over notes and half-steps cross the circle.

"The Circle of Fifths is like a map. The more familiar you are with it, the easier it is to find the places you want to go and even take shortcuts to get there."

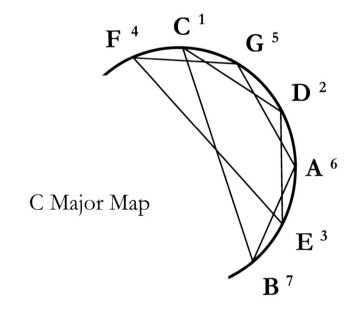

C Major Map

Now, click the mask one hour clockwise. The F goes away and F# appears revealing the notes needed to play a G Major Scale.

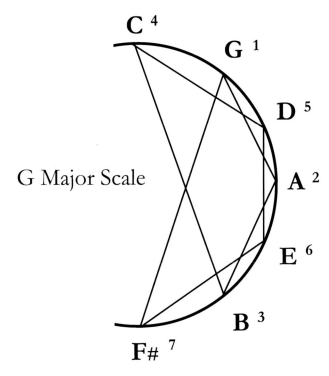

G Major Scale

Each one-hour clockwise click reveals the next Major Scale a fifth interval up. Each one-hour counter-clockwise reveals the next Major Scale a fifth interval down.

"If I know the G Major Scale, then I have the musical neighbors of C Major and D Major under control. I've got six notes out of seven already, and the seventh note will be there if I change it by one half-step."

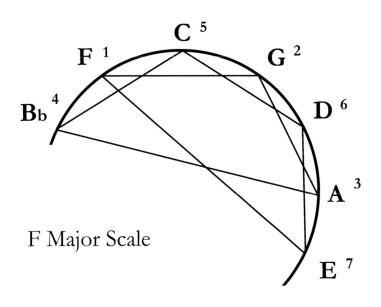

F Major Scale

The Relative Minor Scale

Like most families, scale tones have relatives. In fact, each Major Scale has a *Relative Minor Scale* called the *Natural Minor Scale*. It's easy to see the relationship on the Circle of Fifths.

Learn Twelve Things At Once! As mentioned in Chapter One, *learn one Major Scale and you've learned every Major Scale, that's because they all share the same pattern.* The same is true for the Natural Minor Scale, learn one pattern and apply it to all twelve keys.

Play from the 6th scale degree of the C Major Scale (A) to the A one octave higher. Notice that the *Relative Minor Scale* uses the same notes as its parent Major Scale, it just starts on a different note.

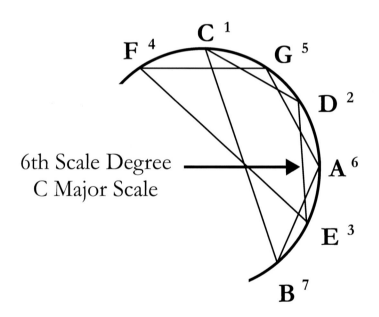

6th Scale Degree
C Major Scale

C Major Scale

C		D		E	F		G		A		B	C
do		re		mi	fa		sol		la		ti	do

A		B	C		D		E	F		G		A
la		ti	do		re		mi	fa		sol		la

A Natural Minor Scale

The diagram below shows the relative minors of all twelve keys. **Try playing the Natural Minor Scale in different keys.**

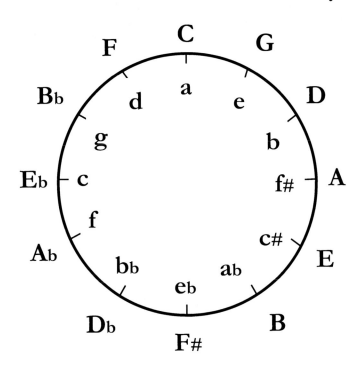

It's Two Scales In One!
Play up from the 6th degree of the Major Scale in any key and you will find that key's relative minor scale. The Major Scale and the Natural Minor Scale each contain the same notes.

Relative Minor Keys (inside of circle)

Get the sound of the Natural Minor Scale in your head and it will serve you well as you progress to the subject of Modal Scales.

With just a few examples you've seen how the Circle of Fifths can instantly reveal the notes in every Major and natural minor scale. You'll find it can be used to map natural chord progressions, transpose from one key to another easily, and provide musical insights that make understanding and playing music simpler. The key, however, is to apply your discoveries to your instrument.

The Circle of Fifths is not music; it is usually just a piece of paper. No music will come from its study unless you play the notes.

"If you make the initial effort (to learn scales) it will come easier and faster and it will give you the confidence and enthusiasm to dig deeper and take it one more notch."

The Modes
Scales a la mode!

"Don't let the word 'mode' bother you. It just means a style of doing something. The French phrase 'a la mode' means 'in fashion.'"

The *Greek Modes* are a family of seven scales. They sound similar to Major and minor scales, but most have altered notes not found in Major/minor scales. The Major Scale is called the *Ionian Mode*. The Ionian mode is the "parent" scale from which the other modal scales are derived. The Modal Scales use the same principal as the Diatonic Chords. Each Modal Scale starts with a different root note from the parent scale.

C Ionian
Major Scale

1	C		D		E	F		G		A		B	C

The Dorian Mode starts on the **2nd** Major Scale degree and uses the same parent scale notes. Songs written in the Dorian mode have a natural minor scale quality, yet, the addition of the sharped 6th note adds a lilt not found in the natural minor scale. Irish fiddle tunes utilize the Dorian mode extensively.

D Dorian
Natural Minor #6th

2	D		E	F		G		A		B	C		D

The *Phrygian Mode* begins on the **3rd** Major Scale degree. It also has an underlying minor scale quality, but the addition of the flat 2nd not found in the minor scale pattern gives the Phrygian mode a feeling of intensity. Spanish flamenco music is a good example of music written in the Phrygian mode.

E Phrygian
Natural Minor b2nd

3	E	F		G		A		B	C		D		E

The *Lydian Mode* begins on the **4th** Major Scale degree. This mode creates a Major Scale pattern with a sharped 4th note. The Lydian mode possesses a lyrical, feminine sounding quality.

F Lydian
Major Scale #4th

The *Mixolydian Mode* begins on the **5th** Major Scale degree. It's a Major Scale pattern with a flatted 7th note. Many popular fiddle tunes including *Old Joe Clark, Salt Creek,* and *Red-Haired Boy* are Mixolydian mode tunes.

G Mixolydian
Major Scale ♭7th

The *Aeolian Mode* is known as the *Natural Minor Scale.* Songs written in the Aeolian mode have a gentle or melancholy feeling. As mentioned earlier, you can play the Natural Minor Scale pattern by starting on the **6th** scale degree of the parent Major Scale.

A Aeolian
Natural Minor Scale

The last of the Greek modes is the *Locrian Mode* which begins on the **7th** Major Scale degree. The Locrian mode has an unsettling sound because it's the only mode that has a flatted 5th chord tone. You won't find many songs written in this mode.

B Locrian
Natural minor ♭2nd-♭5th

Each of the modal scales is named for the note it starts on; C Ionian, D Dorian, etc. In the key of G, for example, the first modal scale is G Ionian, then A Dorian, etc.

The Modal Scales are based on the same principal as the Diatonic Chords; using the parent scale notes and ascending from a new root note each time. The notes altered in each Modal Scale consist mostly of non-diatonic chord tones (1-3-5). The Ionian (I) is the Major Scale pattern, and the Aeolian (VI) is the minor scale pattern, but the other modal scales are Major/minor scale patterns with alterations on the 2nd, 4th, 6th & 7th scale degrees (except the Locrian which also has the flatted 5th). Therefore, we refer to them not as Major and minor scales but as Modal Scales.

Modal Scales Solfege (Diatonic Scales)

Ionian	**do**		re		mi	fa		sol		la		ti	do
Dorian	**re**		mi	fa		sol		la		ti	do		re
Phrygian	**mi**	fa		sol		la		ti	do		re		mi
Lydian	**fa**		sol		la		ti	do		re		mi	fa
Mixolydian	**sol**		la		ti	do		re		mi	fa		sol
Aeolian	**la**		ti	do		re		mi	fa		sol		la
Locrian	**ti**	do		re		mi	fa		sol		la		ti

Consult the partial Circle of Fifths below and you'll see that six of the seven notes of the Major Scale are grouped together neatly with their associated modal scale quality.

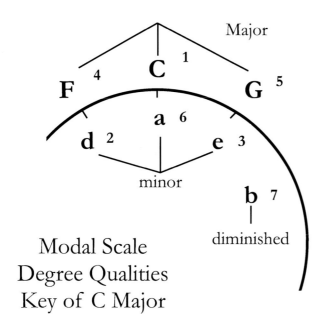

Modal Scale
Degree Qualities
Key of C Major

Row, Row, Row The Modes
Play *Row, Row, Row Your Boat* in each of the seven modes. Just start the tune on a new root each time (see appendix).

Notice the C, F and G notes on the outside of the circle reflect the Major scale chord qualities of those scale degrees in the key of C Major, while the a, d and e notes reflect the minor scale chord qualities. The chord quality of b in the C Major scale is the only oddball, being neither Major nor minor, but diminished (1-b3-b5).

Remember, **Modal Scales contain only Major Scale notes.** Play the same Major Scale notes you already know, in order, starting on a new root note each time, and you have learned to play modal scales. It works in any key!

Three Great Reasons To Know The Modes
1: Understand Major/minor scale relationships.
2: Starting point for study outside the Major Scale.
3: Speak Greek!

Transposing Modes

There are a number of ways to go about transposing modal scales into the parent key (C Ionian, C Dorian, etc.).

Take C Dorian. It can be viewed as a C natural minor scale with a #6th, or a C Major Scale with a ♭3rd & ♭7th, or a B♭ Major Scale starting on C. All three are exactly the same pattern containing the same notes.

C Dorian
C Natural Minor
Scale #6th

C Dorian
C Major Scale ♭3rd/♭7th

C Dorian
B♭ Major Scale starting on 2nd scale degree (C)

Another way to look at transposing is backwards down the scale. Since the Dorian mode starts on the 2nd scale degree, count backward a Major 2nd from the key you want to be in, C for example, and you land on B♭, the scale needed to play in C Dorian. For C Phrygian count down a Major 3rd to A♭, Lydian a Perfect 4th to G, etc.

There are oftentimes a number of ways to understand the same musical concepts. Choose the best way for you.

Julie Andrews didn't get hung up thinking about the modal scales. She hiked to an alpine meadow and sang them!

When thinking about musical ideas becomes too much *thinking*, always remember, these modal sounds can be easily sorted out by the ear. This goes back to the premise that we already know these sounds instinctively.

Since our ears are so used to the sound of the Major Scale, the easiest way to transpose the modes into any key may be the Major Scale method. Just familiarize yourself with the Major Scale notes that need to be altered when transposing into each of the different modal scales. The diagram below will aid in that process.

Pop Quiz
What are the notes of the **C Phrygian scale**?

Answer:
The notes of a C Major Scale: C-D-E-F-G-A-B-C, with a flatted 2nd, 3rd, 6th & 7th: C-Db-Eb-F-G-Ab-Bb-C. These are the same notes found in the Ab Major Scale.

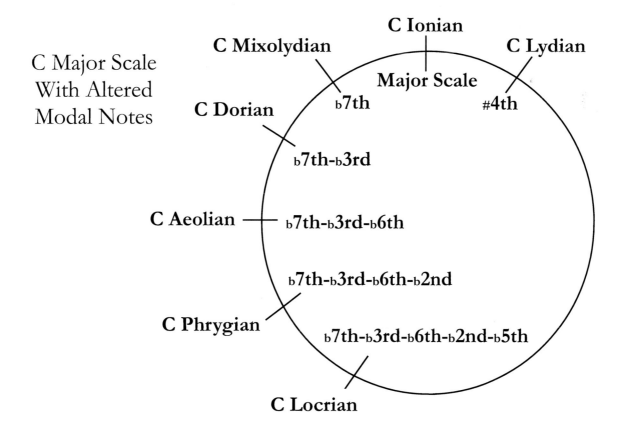

C Major Scale With Altered Modal Notes

C Ionian — Major Scale
C Mixolydian — b7th
C Lydian — #4th
C Dorian — b7th-b3rd
C Aeolian — b7th-b3rd-b6th
C Phrygian — b7th-b3rd-b6th-b2nd
C Locrian — b7th-b3rd-b6th-b2nd-b5th

The Tri-Tone
Tension & Resolution

Uptight people need to relieve tension. Uptight chords do too. In most songs the five-chord (V) is usually written as a *Dominant Seventh Chord* (V7). Changing a V Chord to a V7 chord introduces a tension which makes the V7 Chord sound as if it wants to move to another, more relaxing, chord.

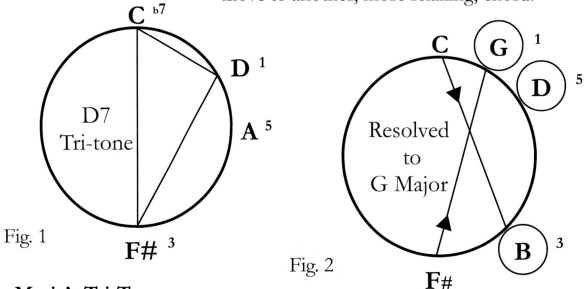

Fig. 1

Fig. 2

Maria's Tri-Tone
Want to write an intense love song? Use the Tri-tone! *Maria* from *West Side Story* does just that: **Do, Fi-Sol**...

In the key of G, for example, the chord built on D is a D7 chord. A full D7 chord contains the notes D-F#-A-C. The F# and C notes are directly opposite each other on the circle (Fig. 1). **Play those two notes together and you'll hear the dissonant sound they produce.** Now, add a D note and play the D7 chord. It sounds a lot more musical, but there exists a dynamic tension that needs resolution.

The resolution to all this musical tension occurs when the two dissonant notes (F# & C) resolve one half-step each (F# to G, and C to B, as in Fig. 2). The result is a resolution back to the home chord of G Major (G-B-D).

These opposition notes (F# & C) are the *Tri-tone* sound of the D7. Any two notes directly opposed to each other on the circle will produce this tension-filled sound.

So, why is it called a Tri-tone? There are three (tri) whole steps from F# to C and three whole steps from C to F# (Fig. 3).

Find any pair of F# & C notes on your instrument and you have the makings of a D7 chord. That dissonance is the essence of the Dominant 7th, or Tri-tone sound. Now, click your Tri-Tonian Triangle counter-clockwise one notch and make a G7th. You'll find the notes needed for Dominant Sevenths everywhere on your instrument.

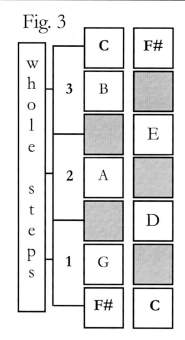

Fig. 3

"The reason for the tension in a Dominant Seventh Chord is there are two notes in there that do not get along. They are not good musical neighbors as they are opposed to each other on the circle and they fight."

G7 - C Major Resolution

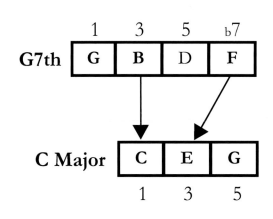

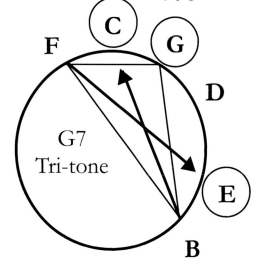

The Pentatonic Scale
The Five-Tone Scale

G Major
Pentatonic Map

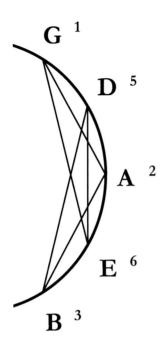

"This Pentatonic, or short scale, is widely used in folk, jazz and oriental music. Using the pentatonic scale we never run the risk of landing on a note that makes it seems like the chord wants to change. It's a very restful scale."

Many two-chord songs often sound as if they have only one chord. These songs lack the musical motivation to move to another chord.

The reason for this chordal lethargy is the melody notes of these songs come from the five-tone *Pentatonic Scale*; a scale which eliminates the tension and resolution factor of a Dominant Seventh Chord by simply leaving out the fourth and seventh notes of the Major Scale.

You'll remember from the previous chapter that Dominant Seventh Chords are built by using the root along with two notes of that key's Major Scale which are directly opposite each other on the Circle of Fifths.

The two notes in opposition provide the tension that makes the Dominant Seventh want to resolve back to the tonic chord. By masking out the two active notes in a D7 chord (C & F#) on the Circle of Fifths, what's left are all the notes needed to create a G Major Pentatonic Scale.

G Major
Pentatonic Scale

1		2		3			5		6		1
Do		Re		Mi			Sol		La		Do
G		A		B			D		E		G

Ascending from the sixth note of a Major Scale results in that key's *Relative Minor* (even though the Pentatonic is a five note scale the notes still retain their original scale degree number). In the G Major Pentatonic Scale when you start on the E and ascend, the result is an E Minor 7th sound. In essence, the G Pentatonic Scale contains two chord sounds, G Major 6th, and E Minor 7th.

1			♭3		4		5			♭7		1
Do			may		Fa		Sol			tay		Do
E			G		A		B			D		E

E minor Pentatonic Scale

The Shortcut To The Blues

To hear G Minor or G Blues sounds flat the 3rd note of the G Scale (B to B♭). Consult the Circle of Fifths and you'll notice the relative minor of B♭ is G. Play a B♭ Pentatonic Scale (B♭-C-D-F-G) and G minor and G blues sounds are immediately at your fingertips.

"In the key of G, to play blues, I need the minor note, B♭, and I also need the ♭7 note, F. I use the B♭ Pentatonic Scale (it has the two notes I need) and play it against a G Major Chord. This is the shortcut to the blues."

G Pentatonic Scale

B♭ Pentatonic Scale

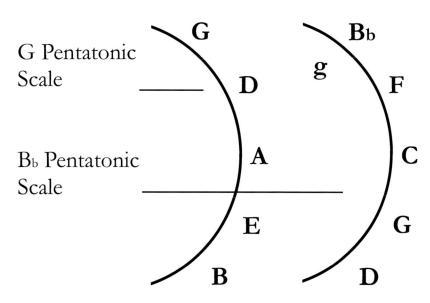

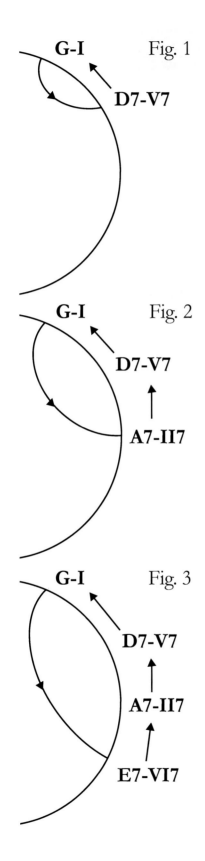

G-I   Fig. 1
D7-V7

G-I   Fig. 2
D7-V7
A7-II7

G-I   Fig. 3
D7-V7
A7-II7
E7-VI7

Chord Progressions
Resolving Around The Circle

As we've learned, we can motivate chords to move logically around the Circle of Fifths using Dominant Seventh chords. In the key of G, the D7 chord wants to resolve counter-clockwise back home to G. This counter-clockwise resolution works all the way around the circle.

These naturally resolving chords are the foundation on which most song progressions are based. **Play through progressions 1 through 4.**

| I | V7 | I | | | Fig. 1 |

| I | II7 | V7 | I | | Fig. 2 |

| I | VI7 | II7 | V7 | I | Fig. 3 |

| I | III7 | VI7 | II7 | V7 | I | Fig. 4 |

Now, play the progressions with an added Four-Chord (IV).

| I | IV | I | V7 | I | Fig. 5 |

| I | IV | VI7 | II7 | V7 | I |

These are the chord progressions to actual songs. As you play these progressions, hum along with the changes and see what songs come to mind.

Try substituting minor chords in these progressions also. You'll remember from the chapter on the modes, the ii, iii, & vi chords lend themselves nicely to this change.

"This is like practicing thousands of songs in advance!"

I	ii7	V7	I

I	vi7	ii7	V7	I

I	iii7	vi7	ii7	V7	I

I	IV	I	ii7	V7	I

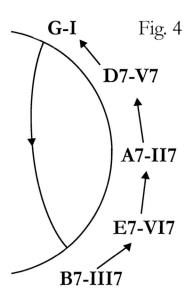

Fig. 4

Get a songbook of popular favorites. Find the songs you already know and play through them humming the melody. This affords you the chance to experiment with playing these progressions in keys that match your voice. Below are a few examples to try.

I	V7	I

Go Tell Aunt Rhody
Skip To My Lou
Down In The Valley

I	IV	I	V7	I

On Top of Old Smokey
Michael, Row the Boat Ashore
This Land Is Your Land

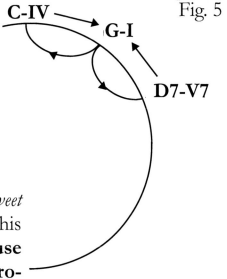

Fig. 5

Many tunes of the 1920's and 30's like *Sweet Georgia Brown* and *Five-Foot-Two* use this resolving 7ths concept. **The reason we use Roman numerals to name these progressions is to make it easier to transpose them to other keys.**

Investigating *The*
Pink Panther
You can uncover the
theme from *The Pink
Panther* by investigat-
ing the Harmonic
Minor Scale.
Here's a clue:
Do, Re-May, **Ti**-Do-
Re-May-Lay-Sol...

Minor Scales
The Natural, Harmonic & Melodic

Let's use the Major Scale pattern to reveal the patterns of the *Natural, Harmonic,* and *Melodic Minor Scales*. As mentioned in the *Circle of Fifths* chapter, the *Natural Minor Scale* pattern lays out naturally when you ascend any Major Scale from the 6th scale degree.

Major Scale from 6th

la		ti	do		re		mi	fa		sol		la

Now that the pattern is revealed we can insert the Natural Minor Scale solfege syllables beginning with Do.

Natural Minor Scale (minor scale solfege)

do		re	may		fa		sol	lay		tay		do

Sharping the 7th scale degree in the Natural Minor Scale pattern creates the *Harmonic Minor Scale* pattern. This introduces the Fa to Ti Tri-tone relationship used to create the V7 chord which resolves back to the Do minor chord.

Harmonic Minor Scale

do		re	may		fa		sol	lay			ti	do

Sharp the 6th note of the Harmonic Minor Scale and you've got the pattern of the ascending *Melodic Minor* scale. Another way to view the ascending Melodic Minor scale is as a Major Scale with a flatted 3rd.

Melodic Minor Scale (ascending)

do		re	may		fa		sol		la		ti	do

Descending this scale reverts to the Natural Minor form.

Melodic Minor (descending)

do		tay		lay	sol		fa		may	re		do

Play through these patterns and give your ears a feel for the scale tones and their related chords. Yours ears will confirm how closely related these three minor scale patterns are to the Major Scale.

Finally, don't think of minor scales as isolated entities to be memorized separately, but subtle shifts in Major Scale thinking. And remember, there's only one Major Scale pattern!

The key to understanding the usage of these minor scales, or any of the other musical concepts presented in this book, is to play them, listen to what they sound like, and experiment where you can use the sounds in songs.

Summary

Exercising and training the ears and hands will allow you to apply the knowledge presented in this book to your instrument. The final step is to get out of the way.

You can't think your way through a tune, you have to hear it, play it; listen to it as it comes out. Trust your hands and ears to do the job you've trained them for.

One way to practice getting the thinking out of your playing is to sing, hum, or scat along with the music as you play. This gives your mind something constructive to occupy itself with while you are having fun not thinking!

When you get to this point (and you will) music will flow from you effortlessly.

Questions?

If you have any questions concerning the material presented in the book please visit our website @ www.naturalwaymusic .com and email us your question(s).

Appendix

3 Appendix

In this section of the book you'll find many useful tools to aid in the discovery of your own music. First, you'll find a handy reference guide to the most widely used western scales followed by the sharp and flat Major Scale keys.

Next is a page of **scales & arpeggios**. Spend some time playing the notes in these scales & arpeggios and listen as familiar tunes literally start dropping out. It's also a great idea to use a metronome during your practice. Steady rhythm is a cornerstone of solid musicianship.

The bulk of the appendix consists of **solfege examples** which have been referred to earlier in the book. The solfege syllables are curious things. Invest the time in them and one day you'll realize you are hearing in a new and improved fashion thanks to them. The **Holiday Tune Section** is a lot of fun because the notes in those tunes are so easily recognizable.

And finally, if you are interested in learning to read standard music notation, we've included a page that may be helpful in that endeavor.

Major League Mozart
If you've ever been to a Major League Baseball game you know the fans love arpeggios as much as Mozart did. In fact, notes from his Eine kleine Nachtmusik; **Sol**-Do, **Sol**-Do, **Sol**-Do-Sol-Do-Mi-Sol...are played at most every game; **Sol**-Do-Mi-Sol, Mi-Sol...Charge!

Popular Scale Patterns

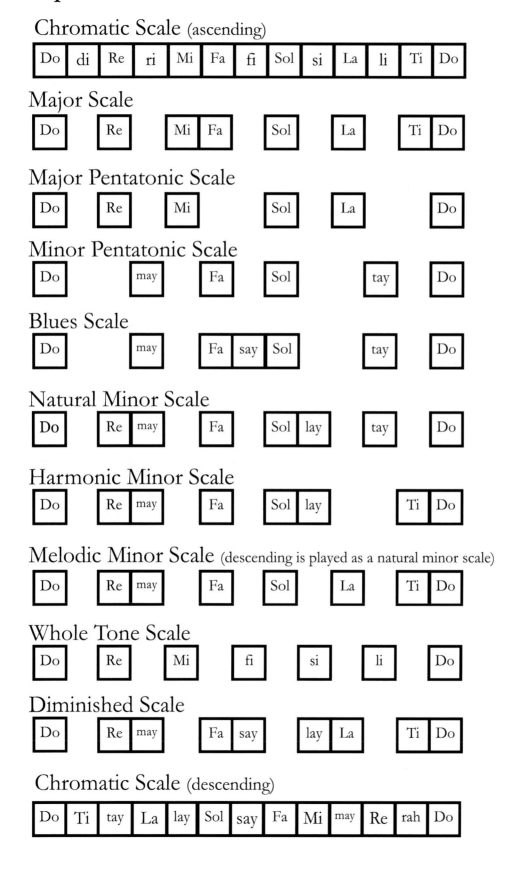

Chromatic Scale (ascending)

| Do | di | Re | ri | Mi | Fa | fi | Sol | si | La | li | Ti | Do |

Major Scale

| Do | | Re | | Mi | Fa | | Sol | | La | | Ti | Do |

Major Pentatonic Scale

| Do | | Re | | Mi | | | Sol | | La | | | Do |

Minor Pentatonic Scale

| Do | | may | | Fa | | Sol | | | tay | | Do |

Blues Scale

| Do | | may | | Fa | say | Sol | | | tay | | Do |

Natural Minor Scale

| Do | | Re | may | | Fa | | Sol | lay | | tay | | Do |

Harmonic Minor Scale

| Do | | Re | may | | Fa | | Sol | lay | | | Ti | Do |

Melodic Minor Scale (descending is played as a natural minor scale)

| Do | | Re | may | | Fa | | Sol | | La | | Ti | Do |

Whole Tone Scale

| Do | | Re | | Mi | | fi | | si | | li | | Do |

Diminished Scale

| Do | | Re | may | | Fa | say | | lay | La | | Ti | Do |

Chromatic Scale (descending)

| Do | Ti | tay | La | lay | Sol | say | Fa | Mi | may | Re | rah | Do |

Introduction of Flats

Key of C (no flats or sharps)

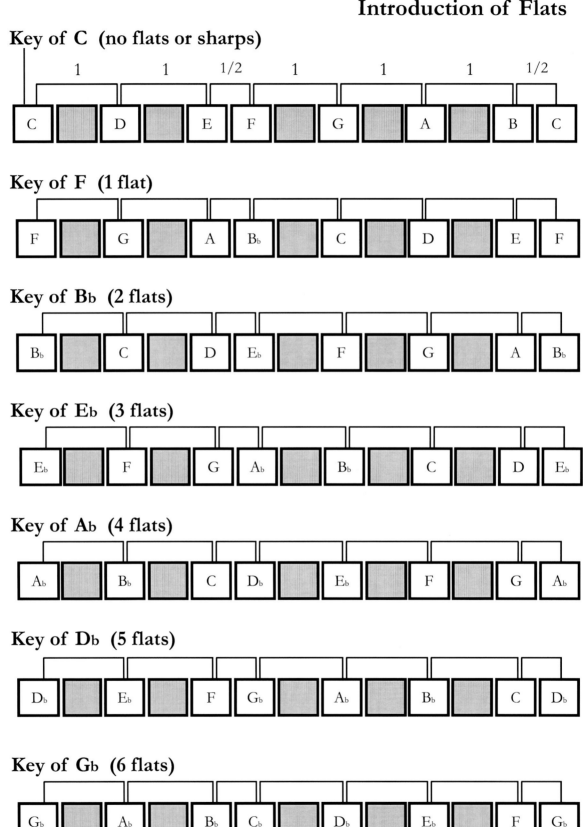

Introduction of Sharps

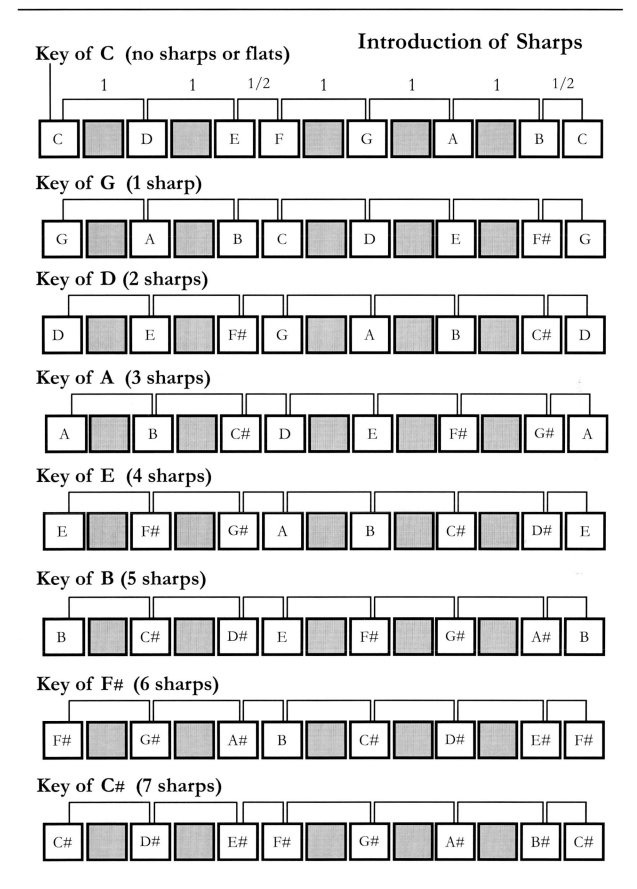

Scales & Arpeggios
Practice playing the following scales and arpeggios, both up and down, in all keys. You may be surprised how many songs drop right out of these patterns. This is also great ear-training.

Italian Lesson
When you play the notes of a chord in succession, instead of all at once, it's called an *Arpeggio* (ahr-PED-joh): Do-Mi-Sol-Do.

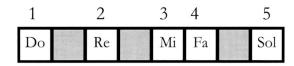

1st 5 Major Scale Notes

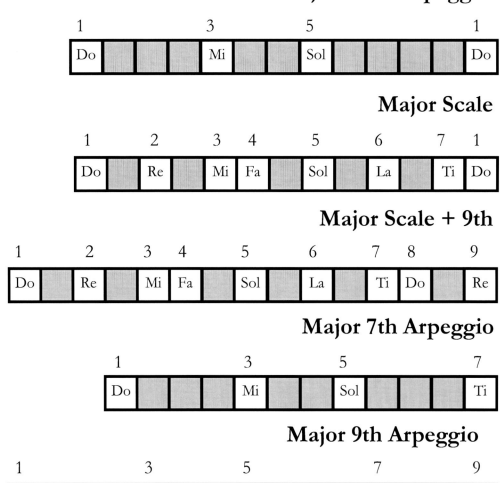

Major Scale Arpeggio

Major Scale

Major Scale + 9th

Major 7th Arpeggio

Major 9th Arpeggio

Solfege Songs

A practical approach to learning songs is to first know the chord changes. Most songs are made up of one progression that is repeated. Look for the patterns. Once you can comfortably play the chords you can find the melody notes of the tune. A good deal of the time the melody notes are contained in the associated chord. Chords are great place to look for the melody. Put the chord changes and melody together and presto, you are playing the song. Also, when learning a new tune, don't just learn it in one area of your instrument. Try playing the tune in a different octave for example. Remember also to always play in time. Practicing with a metronome, or drum machine is an invaluable way to hone your rhythmic skills. Above all, have fun playing!

Sing and play the following familiar songs using the solfege syllables. Syllables with dashes between them are sung in quick succession, while the commas denote short pauses between the notes. Syllables in bold italic (***Do***) are sung one octave higher, and those simply in bold (**Do**) are sung one octave lower. We have not written out each tune in its entirety. Let your ears find the rest of the notes.

Star Spangled Banner
Sol-Mi Do Mi Sol ***Do***...
O-oh say can you see...

This Land Is Your Land
  Do Re Mi Fa,   Fa,   Fa   Do Re Mi, Mi,
This land is your land, this land is my land,
 Mi Do-Do, Re, Re...
from Cal-i-for-nia...

Down In The Valley
  Sol   Do Re Mi, Do, Mi-Re   Do Re
Down in the val-ley, val-ley so low,
  Sol   **Ti**   Re Fa, Re, **Ti** Do Re Do...
hang your head ov-er, hear the wind blow...

Pop Goes The Weasel
Do, Do-Re,   Re-Mi-Sol-Mi-Do
All   a-round the mul-ber-ry bush,
 Sol-Do Do-Re   Re-Mi, Do...
the monkey chased the weasel...

Worried Man Blues
La Sol, Sol - Sol La   Do, Re Mi, Mi- Mi Re   Do...
It takes a worr-ied man, to sing a worried song...

Home On The Range
Sol   Sol Do Re Mi,   Do-**Ti - La** Fa Fa Fa...
Oh, give me a home where the buff-a-lo roam...

Happy Trails
Sol-Sol   Sol, Sol Mi, **Sol-La, Sol-Li, Sol-Ti**...
Hap-py trails to you, un-til, we meet, again...

Old Joe Clark
Sol La Tay La Sol Fa   Mi, Sol La Tay La Sol...
 I went down to old Joe's house, I slept on the floor...

Oh, Susanna
Do-Re Mi   Sol Sol, La-Sol Mi Do, Re-Mi Mi Re Do Re...
Well I come from Al - a - bama with a banjo on my knee...

Ode to Joy (Instrumental)
Mi Mi Fa Sol Sol Fa Mi Re Do Do Re Mi Mi, Re-Re...

Mary Had A Little Lamb
Mi Re Do Re Mi Mi Mi, Re Re Re,   Mi Sol Sol,
Ma-ry had a lit-tle lamb, lit-tle lamb, lit-tle lamb...

Happy Birthday
Sol-Sol La Sol Do **Ti, Sol-Sol La Sol** Re Do,
Hap-py birth-day to you, hap-py birth-day to you...

Brother John (Frère Jacques)
Do Re Mi Do Do Re Mi Do
Are you sleeping, are you sleeping
Mi-Fa Sol, Mi-Fa Sol...
Brother John, Brother John...

Camptown Races
Sol Sol Mi Sol La Sol Mi, Mi Re, Mi Re...
Camptown la-dies sing this song, do-dah, do-dah...

Home Sweet Home
Do-Re Mi, Fa La Sol, Mi Sol Fa, Mi-Fa Re Mi...
Be it ev-er so hum-ble there's no, place like home...

Grandfather's Clock
Sol Sol Do, **Ti** Do Re, Do Re Mi, Fa Mi **La**...
Well my grand-fath-er's clock was too large for the shelf...

Three Blind Mice
Mi Re Do, Mi Re Do,
Three blind mice, three blind mice,
Sol Fa-Fa Mi, Sol Fa-Fa Mi...
See how they run, see how they run...

Holiday Tunes

Joy To The World
Do, Ti La-Sol,   Fa-Mi   Re, Do
Joy to the world, the Lord has come
Sol-La,   La-Ti,   Ti-***Do***...
Let earth re-ceive her king...

I Heard The Bells (It Came Upon A Midnight Clear)
Sol Mi,   **Ti** Re-Do **La Sol,   La Sol**
  I   heard the bel-ls   on Christ-mas morn...

Jingle Bells
Mi Mi Mi,   Mi Mi Mi,   Mi Sol Do Re Mi…
Jingle bells, jingle bells, jingle all the way...

Silent Night
Sol, La-Sol   Mi, Sol, La-Sol Mi,
 Si—l—ent night, ho—l—y   night,
Re, Re Ti,   ***Do, Do*** Sol…
All is calm, all   is bright...

Deck The Halls
  Sol, Fa-Mi   Re   Do   Re Mi Do...
Deck the halls with boughs of hol-ly…

Auld Lange Syne
 Sol   Do, **Ti**—Do Mi Re, Do-Re...
Should old ac-quain-tance be for-got...

DO, RE, MI, (Doe a Deer) SOLFEGE SYLLABLES

1   2 3   1   3   1   3
do, re mi, do mi, do mi.

2 3 4 4   3 2 4
re, mi-fa-fa-mi-re fa.

3   4 5   3 5   3 5
mi, fa-sol, mi-sol, mi sol.

4   5 6 6 5 4 6
fa, sol-la-la, sol-fa la.

5   1 2 3 4 5 6
sol, do-re-mi-fa-sol-la.

6 2 3 4 5   6 7
la, re-mi-fa-sol-la-ti.

7 3 4 5 6 7 8
ti, mi-fa-sol-la-ti-do.

8 76 4 7 5 8 5 3 2 1
do-ti-la, fa, ti sol, do, sol-mi-re-do!

ROW, ROW, ROW YOUR BOAT
SOLFEGE SYLLABLES

Ionian

1 1 1 2 -3

do, do, do, re-mi

3 2 - 3 4 - 5

mi, re-mi, fa-sol.

8 - 8 - 8

do-do-do

5 - 5 - 5

sol-sol-sol

3 - 3 - 3

mi-mi-mi

1 - 1 - 1

do-do-do

Descending Arpeggio (Broken Chord)

5 4 3 2 1

sol, fa-mi, re-do!

ROW, ROW, ROW YOUR BOAT
Modal Solfege Syllables

Dorian	**Phrygian**	**Lydian**
2 2 2 3 4	3 3 3 4 5	4 4 4 5 6
re, re, re, mi-fa,	mi, mi, mi, fa-sol,	fa, fa, fa, sol-la,
4 3 4 5 6	5 4 5 6 7	6 5 6 7 8
fa-mi, fa-sol, la.	sol-fa, sol-la, ti.	la-sol, la-ti, do.
9 9 9	10 10 10	11 11 11
re-re-re.	mi-mi-mi.	fa-fa-fa.
6 6 6	7 7 7	8 8 8
la-la-la.	ti-ti-ti.	do-do-do.
4 4 4	5 5 5	6 6 6
fa-fa-fa.	sol-sol-sol.	la-la-la.
2 2 2	3 3 3	4 4 4
re-re-re.	mi-mi-mi.	fa-fa-fa.
6 5 4 3 2	7 6 5 4 3	8 7 6 5 4
la-sol, fa-mi, re.	ti-la, sol-fa, mi.	do-ti, la-sol, fa.

ROW, ROW, ROW YOUR BOAT
Modal Solfege Syllables

Mixolydian	Aeolian	Locrian
5 5 5 6 7	6 6 6 7 8	7 7 7 8 9
sol, sol, sol, la-ti,	la, la, la, ti-do,	ti,ti,ti, do-re,
7 6 7 8 9	8 7 8 9 10	9 8 9 10 11
ti-la, ti-do, re.	do-ti, do-re, mi.	re-do, re-mi, fa.
12 12 12	13 13 13	14 14 14
sol-sol-sol.	la -la -la.	ti -ti -ti.
9 9 9	10-10-10.	11 11 11
re-re-re.	mi-mi-mi.	fa-fa-fa.
7 7 7	8 8 8	9 9 9
ti-ti-ti.	do-do-do.	re-re-re.
5 5 5	6 6 6	7 7 7
sol-sol-sol.	la-la-la.	ti-ti-ti.
9 8 7 6 5	10 9 8 7 6	11 10 9 8 7
re-do, ti-la, sol.	mi-re, do-ti, la..	fa-mi, re-do, ti.

A Note On Notation

For those interested in learning to read standard music notation, the relationship between the *Grand Staff* and the modes is illustrated in the diagram below.

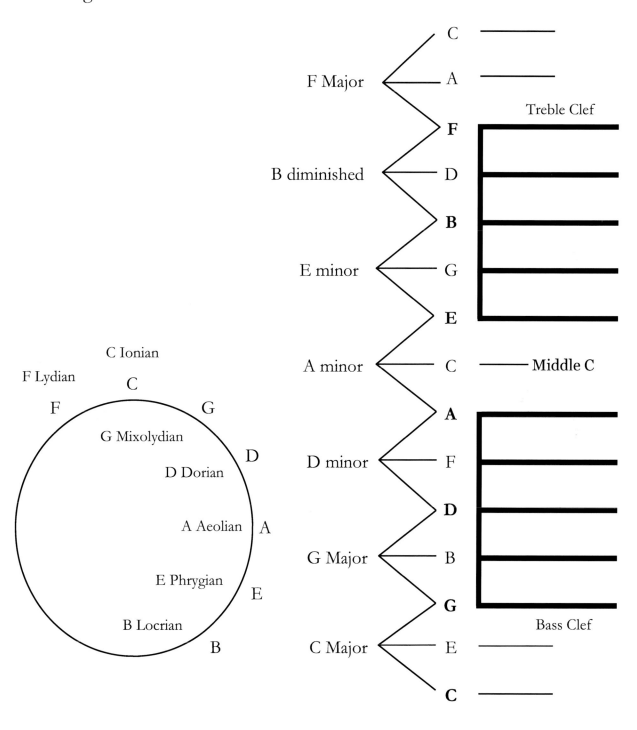

Glossary

Accidentals: Sharp, Flat and Natural signs used to raise, lower, or return a note to its normal pitch.

Arpeggio: The notes of a chord played in succession, i.e. broken chord.

Augmented: Raising the fourth or fifth chord tone by one half-step.

Diatonic Scale: Another name for Major Scale (ditonic).

Chord: Three or more notes sounded at the same time.

Chord Inversion: A chord with a bass note other than its root (3-5-1, 5-1-3).

Chord Progression: Movement from one chord to another.

Circle of Fifths: Keys or chords arranged around a circle in fifth intervals.

Diminished: Lowering the fifth chord tone by one half-step.

Dominant: Fifth scale degree of a diatonic scale.

Dominant Seventh: Chord built using the 1st, 3rd, 5th and b7th scale degrees.

Enharmonic: Two notes of the same pitch written differently (B#/C).

Equilateral Triangle: Triangle with all sides equal.

Flat: To lower a note one half-step.

Half-Tone (half-step): The smallest interval, one half-step (minor 2nd).

Interval: The distance between two notes.

Key: The tonal center or tonic note of a scale.

Key Signature: Number of sharps or flats notated on a piece of written music to indicate the key.

Major Scale: A diatonic scale with half-steps occurring between the third and fourth, and seventh and eighth scale degrees.

Modal Scales: Greek scales using diatonic scale notes arranged in specific interval patterns.

Octave: The interval between the first and eighth scale degrees.

Pentatonic Scale: Five-note scale which eliminates the 4th and 7th scale degrees of a diatonic scale.

Pitch: The highness, or lowness of a note's vibrating frequency.

Relative Keys: Major and minor keys that share the same key signature.

Root: First note of a scale (also called *tonic* or *home note*).

Scalene Triangle: Triangle with no equal sides (Tri-tonian Triangle).

Sharp: To raise a note one half-step.

Solfege: Do, re, mi, etc., single syllables used to sing the notes of a scale.

Subdominant: Fourth scale degree of a diatonic scale.

Tetrachord: A four-note element, two of which constitute a scale.

Tonic: First note of a scale (also called *root* or *home note*).

Transposing: Changing from one key to another.

Triad: Three note chord consisting of the root, third, and fifth scale degrees.

Tri-tone: Interval of three whole tones (augmented 4th-diminished 5th).

Unison: Two or more notes sounding at the same pitch.

Whole-Tone (whole-step): Interval consisting of two half-steps (Major 2nd).

Suggested Reading

Ashton, Anthony. *Harmonograph: A Visual Guide To The Mathematics Of Music.* New York, NY: Walker Publishing Company, Inc., 2003. ISBN: 0-8027-1409-9

Coker, Jerry. *Improvising Jazz.* New York, NY: Simon & Schuster, 1964. ISBN: 0-671-62829-1

Jeans, James. *Science & Music.* New York, NY: Dover Publications, 1968. ISBN: 0-486-61964-8.

Judy, Stephanie. *Making Music For The Joy Of It: Enhancing Creativity, Skills, and Musical Confidence.* New York, NY: G. P. Putnam's Sons, 1990. ISBN: 0-87477-593-0.

Mathieu, W.A. *Harmonic Experience: Tonal Harmony From Its Natural Origins To Its Modern Experience.* Rochester, VT: Inner Traditions International, 1997. ISBN: 0-89281-560-4.

Rubenstein, Ed. *An Awakening From The Trances Of Everyday Life: A Journey To Empowerment.* Marshall, NC: Sages Way Press, 1999. ISBN: 0-9668700-0-X.

Schneider, Michael S. *A Beginner's Guide to Constructing the Universe: The Mathematical Archetypes of Nature, Art and Science, A Voyage From One to Ten.* New York, NY: Harper Perennial, 1994. ISBN: 0-06-092671-6.

Shanet, Howard. *Learn to Read Music.* New York, NY: Simon & Schuster, 1956. Library of Congress Catalog Card Number: 55-11046.

Werner, Kenny. *Effortless Mastery: Liberating The Master Musician Within.* New Albany, IN: Jamey Aebersold Jazz, 1996. ISBN: 1-56224-003-X.

About The Authors

Jim D'Ville's professional career included many years of listening to records as a radio disc jockey and wondering what in the world musicians were doing. He began learning to play the banjo at the age of 34 having had no previous musical training other than two failed music theory courses. In his attempt to understand the instrument, Jim began searching out instructional materials for the 5-string banjo. To his surprise, there was scant information to be found on music theory as it related to the banjo. In 1994, Jim took a workshop taught by Bill Keith. That workshop opened the door to the musical universe.

After about three years of study, Jim approached Bill about working together on an easy to understand music instruction book based on his approach to practical music theory. The result is the book you are now reading.

Jim currently plays, studies and teaches ukulele on the Oregon coast.

Bill Keith's parents have said Bill began *playing* at a very early age "on the linoleum." Bill went on to play ukulele, piano, tenor banjo, and finally 5-string banjo (he has also played pedal steel guitar).

His innovations and contributions to the music world are staggering. He pioneered a completely new style of banjo playing, now called "melodic" or Keith style. Bill co-wrote the most popular banjo instruction book to date with Earl Scruggs, in addition to authoring the first banjo instruction manuals in French and Italian. He invented the Keith tuning pegs and took the banjo to musical vistas never before imagined. Bill has also taught hundreds of workshops all over the world.

His performance credits include touring and/or recording with Bill Monroe & The Bluegrass Boys, Jim Kweskin & The Jug Band, Judy Collins, Muleskinner, Ian & Sylvia, Jonathan Edwards, and Richard Greene & The Grass Is Greener.

Bill lives in upstate New York.